CABO VERDE

CABO VERDE 2016 HUMAN RIGHTS REPORT

EXECUTIVE SUMMARY

The government of Cabo Verde is a parliamentary representative democratic republic, largely modeled on the Portuguese system. Constitutional powers are shared between the head of state, President Jorge Carlos Fonseca, and head of government, Prime Minister Ulisses Correia e Silva. The Supreme Court, the National Electoral Commission, and international observers declared the 2016 nationwide legislative elections generally free and fair.

Civilian authorities at times did not maintain effective control over security forces.

The most serious human rights problems occurred in the following areas: overcrowding of prisons, child abuse, and violence and discrimination against women.

Other human rights problems included excessive force and aggression against persons arrested and detained by police; trafficking in persons, including some instances of child sexual exploitation; and forced child labor.

Although the government took steps to prosecute and punish public officials who committed human rights abuses, the process was lengthy. The National Police took disciplinary action against officers who acted outside the law. The government sometimes downplayed or disregarded police abuses.

Section 1. Respect for the Integrity of the Person, Including Freedom from:

a. Arbitrary Deprivation of Life and other Unlawful or Politically Motivated Killings

There were no reports the government or its agents committed arbitrary or unlawful killings.

b. Disappearance

There were no reports of politically motivated disappearances.

c. Torture and Other Cruel, Inhuman, or Degrading Treatment or Punishment

The constitution and law prohibit such practices. Media, however, continued to cite instances of physical violence. The most common types of abuses were excessive force and aggression against persons arrested and detained by police. In most cases the National Police Council took action against abusers.

Prison and Detention Center Conditions

Prison conditions were harsh and potentially life threatening due to gross overcrowding and inadequate housing and sanitation, mainly at the Central Prison of Praia.

<u>Physical Conditions</u>: There are five prisons in the country; the two largest had populations that substantially exceeded capacity (indicated in parentheses). The Central Prison of Praia (CCP) had 1,110 inmates (880), the Central Prison of Sao Vicente 286 (180), the regional prison of Santo Antao 34 (50), the prison on Sal Island 90 (250), and Fogo 49 (50).

Prisoners also complained about inadequate sanitation, ventilation, lighting, and heating. Conditions in general were inadequate for inmates with mental disabilities or substance addictions. There were too few corrections officers to deal with the growing number of such prisoners. Conditions were markedly better for female prisoners, who generally had significantly more space and better sanitary conditions than male prisoners.

During the year there was one death reported in prison.

The government sent some prisoners to the CCP to separate inmates based on trial status, gender, and age, but there were cases of youths sharing cells with adults.

<u>Administration</u>: The Ministry of Justice, Ministry of Internal Affairs, Cabo Verdean Institute for Gender Equality and Equity--a government agency--and the National Statistics Institute (INE) worked together to establish uniform standards for data collection and recordkeeping.

There were no prison ombudsmen to respond to complaints.

Prisoners' relatives reported complaints, but corrections officials claimed all had been investigated and disproven.

<u>Independent Monitoring</u>: The government permitted formal visits by international human rights monitors to the prisons and individual prisoners. Local nongovernmental organizations (NGOs) and members of the press made frequent visits to prisons to record conditions.

d. Arbitrary Arrest or Detention

The constitution and law prohibit arbitrary arrest and detention, and the government generally observed these prohibitions.

Role of the Police and Security Apparatus

The National Police, under the control of the Ministry of Internal Affairs, is responsible for law enforcement. The Judiciary Police, under the Ministry of Justice, is responsible for major investigations. The armed forces, under the Ministry of Defense, are responsible for protecting the national territory (maritime and terrestrial) and sovereignty of the country. Logistical constraints, including a shortage of vehicles and communications equipment, and poor forensic capacity continued to limit police effectiveness.

Civilian authorities maintained effective control over the armed forces and police (including the Coast Guard, National Guard, National Police, and Judiciary Police), and the government had somewhat effective mechanisms to investigate and punish abuse and corruption.

There were no reports of impunity involving the security forces during the year.

Authorities investigated abuses by police, and most investigations resulted in legal action against those responsible. During the first eight months of the year, the National Police Council received 16 reports of police violence; most cases concerned physical abuse. The National Police Disciplinary Board reviewed the cases.

Arrest Procedures and Treatment of Detainees

The National Police may not make arrests without a warrant issued by the Attorney General's Office, unless police apprehend the person in the act of committing a felony. Neither the National Police nor Judiciary Police have the authority to conduct investigations unless mandated by the Attorney General's Office. Even if there is incriminating evidence, suspected criminals are not arrested until a decision is made by the Attorney General's Office. The law stipulates a suspect must be brought before a judge within 48 hours of arrest. In most cases, however, detainees waited more than 48 hours for their hearings. The law provides a detainee the right to prompt judicial determination of the legality of the detention, and authorities respected this right. Attorneys inform detainees of the charges against them. There is a functioning bail system. Authorities allowed detainees prompt access to family members and to a lawyer of the detainee's choice if the detainee could afford it. For a detainee or family unable to pay, the Cabo Verdean Bar Association appoints a lawyer.

The judicial system was overburdened and understaffed, and criminal cases frequently ended when charges were dropped before a determination of guilt or innocence was made.

<u>Detainee's Ability to Challenge Lawfulness of Detention before a Court</u>: Persons are entitled to challenge in court the legal basis or arbitrary nature of their detention and obtain prompt release and compensation if found to have been unlawfully detained.

e. Denial of Fair Public Trial

The law provides for an independent judiciary, and the government generally respected judicial independence. The judicial system, however, lacked sufficient staffing and was inefficient.

There is a military court, which cannot try civilians. The military court provides the same protections as civil criminal courts.

Trial Procedures

The constitution and law provide for the right to a fair public trial, and an independent judiciary generally enforced this right. Defendants enjoy a presumption of innocence. They have the right to be informed promptly and in detail of the charges, with free interpretation as necessary from the moment charged through all appeals. The law provides for the right to a fair and public nonjury trial without undue delay, but cases often continued for years. Defendants have the right to be present at their trial and to consult with an attorney in a timely manner. Free counsel is provided for the indigent in all types of cases. Defendants have adequate time and facilities to prepare a defense. Defendants and their attorneys have access to government-held evidence relevant to their cases.

Defendants have the right to confront or question witnesses against them and to present witnesses and evidence in their defense; the right not to be compelled to testify or confess guilt; and the right to appeal regional court decisions to the Supreme Court of Justice (SCJ). The law extends the above rights to all citizens.

Political Prisoners and Detainees

There were no reports of political prisoners or detainees.

Civil Judicial Procedures and Remedies

Courts are impartial and independent and handle civil matters including lawsuits seeking damages for, or an injunction ordering the cessation of, a human rights violation. Individuals and organizations may appeal adverse domestic decisions to regional human right bodies. Both administrative and judicial remedies are available.

f. Arbitrary or Unlawful Interference with Privacy, Family, Home, or Correspondence

The constitution and law prohibit such actions, and there were no reports the government failed to respect these prohibitions.

Section 2. Respect for Civil Liberties, Including:

a. Freedom of Speech and Press

The constitution and law provide for freedom of speech and press, and the government generally respected these rights. An independent press, an effective judiciary, and a functioning democratic political system combined to promote freedom of speech and press.

Internet Freedom

The government did not restrict or disrupt access to the internet or censor online content, and there were no credible reports the government monitored private online communications without appropriate legal authority.

According to the Cabo Verdean National Communications Authority's 2016 Second Quarter Report, 59 percent of the population used the internet.

Academic Freedom and Cultural Events

There were no government restrictions on academic freedom or cultural events.

b. Freedom of Peaceful Assembly and Association

The constitution and law provide for the freedoms of assembly and association, and the government generally respected these rights.

c. Freedom of Religion

See the Department of State's *International Religious Freedom Report* at www.state.gov/religiousfreedomreport/.

d. Freedom of Movement, Internally Displaced Persons, Protection of Refugees, and Stateless Persons

The constitution and law provide for freedom of internal movement, foreign travel, emigration, and repatriation, and the government generally respected these rights.

The government cooperated with the Office of the UN High Commissioner for Refugees (UNHCR) and other humanitarian organizations in assisting refugees and asylum seekers.

Protection of Refugees

Access to Asylum: The law does not provide for the granting of asylum or refugee status, and the government has not established a system for providing protection to refugees. The country has not established national legislation or an institutional body for granting asylum or refugee status. While very few asylum applications were registered (UNHCR reported only two cases in total in 2011 and 2012 and none since), the actual number of asylum seekers was unknown, since there is no systematic procedure in place to register and process asylum claims. Because UNHCR does not have an established presence in the country, asylum seekers who request protection and assistance are referred by the International Organization for Migration to UNHCR's regional representation for West Africa in Dakar, Senegal, which conducts refugee status determinations. Temporary protection mechanisms and access to basic services are in place for asylum seekers while they await a decision.

Section 3. Freedom to Participate in the Political Process

The constitution provides citizens the ability to choose their government in free and fair periodic elections held by secret ballot and based on universal and equal suffrage.

Residents who are not Cabo Verdean citizens are able to vote in municipal elections. Any foreigner residing in Cabo Verde for more than three years can vote in municipal elections. Any resident from a member country of the Community of Countries of Portuguese Language (CPLP)--which includes Angola, Brazil, Equatorial Guinea, Guinea-Bissau, Mozambique, Portugal, and Timor-Leste--can vote in municipal elections regardless of how long they have resided in Cabo Verde. Only Cabo Verdean citizens, including those living outside the country, can vote in legislative and presidential elections.

Elections and Political Participation

Recent Elections: In the 2016 legislative elections, individuals and parties were free to declare their candidacies and candidates for a total of 72 seats. The main opposition party, Movement for Democracy (MpD), won 40 seats in the National Assembly with approximately 53 percent of the vote, returning the party to power for the first time in 15 years. The ruling party, African Party for the Independence of Cabo Verde (PAICV), won 29 seats with 37 percent, and the Union for a Democratic and Independent Cabo Verde (UCID) won the remaining three seats with 6 percent. International observers characterized these elections as generally free and fair.

The most recent presidential election took place on October 2. Jorge Carlos Fonseca, the candidate supported by the MpD, won the election with approximately 74 percent of the vote.

Election observers from the African Union and Economic Community of West African States (ECOWAS) characterized these elections as free, transparent, and credible. Observers noted some irregularities, however, including voters being pressured near polling stations to vote for certain candidates and allegations of vote buying.

Participation of Women and Minorities: Male dominance in positions of power continued despite efforts to promote women's advancement.

Women's participation fell in positions within the central government but remained particularly high on the SCJ, and especially in prosecutorial positions. At the local level, however, in community associations and on city councils, women had less representation.

Women held 17 of the 72 National Assembly seats and occupied three of the 11 cabinet-level positions in government ministries. Women filled three of the eight seats on the SCJ, including the presidency, and one female mayor was elected in the 2012 municipal elections.

Section 4. Corruption and Lack of Transparency in Government

The law provides penalties of up to 15 years' imprisonment for corruption by officials, and the government implemented the law effectively. Officials sometimes engaged in corrupt practices with impunity, especially at the municipal level, although there were no new reports of government corruption during the year.

Corruption: Polling released by Afrobarometer in September 2015 showed citizens' perceptions of corruption in the country had risen in comparison with 2013. The study revealed these perceptions of increased corruption extended beyond the National Assembly and other elected bodies to the National Police, which 19 percent of citizens considered corrupt.

Financial Disclosure: The law sets parameters for public officials to submit declarations of interest, income, and family wealth, and regulates public discussion of this information. These declarations should include any asset worth more than 500,000 escudos ($5,043). Failure to submit a declaration may lead to a prohibition on public officials holding office for a period of one to five years. The SCJ must approve public disclosure of the declarations. When involved in criminal cases of alleged corruption, public officials must declare or prove the source of their income or wealth. The SCJ is in charge of monitoring the law and enforcing compliance, but enforcement was poor.

Public Access to Information: The law provides for public access to government information without restriction, provided privacy rights are respected. The government frequently granted access.

Section 5. Governmental Attitude Regarding International and Nongovernmental Investigation of Alleged Violations of Human Rights

A number of domestic and international human rights groups generally operated without government restriction, investigating and publishing their findings on human rights cases. Government officials were somewhat cooperative and responsive to their views.

Section 6. Discrimination, Societal Abuses, and Trafficking in Persons

Women

<u>Rape and Domestic Violence</u>: Rape is a crime punishable by eight to 16 years in prison, and domestic violence is punishable by one to five years in prison. Spousal rape is implicitly covered by the gender-based violence law; penalties range from one to five years' imprisonment. This 2001 law focuses on increasing protection of victims, strengthening penalties for offenders, and raising awareness about gender-based violence. The law calls for establishing several care centers, with financial and management autonomy, but implementation lagged due to inadequate staffing and financial resources. Violence and discrimination against women remained significant problems.

Rede Sol (a network that connects civil society organizations, the National Police, health centers, hospitals, and community law centers) covered 56 percent of the national territory and had representation on seven islands and in 12 of the 22 municipalities. The Ministry of Justice created "casas do direito" (civil rights houses), which serve as public spaces that provide citizens with access to justice and promote civic participation. In 2015 they received reports of 241 cases of gender-based violence nationwide. As of July, 61 cases were reported to the casas do direito.

The government enforced the law against rape and domestic violence effectively.

<u>Sexual Harassment</u>: The criminal code and the law criminalize sexual harassment. Penalties include up to one year in prison and a fine equal to up to two years of the perpetrator's salary. Although authorities generally enforced the law, statistics on prosecutions, convictions, and punishments for sexual harassment were not available. There was no data on the number of cases of sexual harassment during the year. Sexual harassment was common and widely accepted in the culture.

Reproductive Rights: The civil code grants all citizens the freedom to decide the number, spacing, and timing of their children; manage their reproductive health; and have access to the information and means to do so free from discrimination, coercion, or violence. All citizens had access to contraception. Family planning centers throughout the country distributed some contraceptives freely to the public. These centers provided skilled assistance and counseling, both before and after childbirth and in cases of sexually transmitted infections, including HIV. Postnatal services included family planning and free oral/injectable contraceptives. No government policies adversely affect emergency health care, including complications arising from abortion.

Discrimination: The law provides for the same legal status and rights for women as for men. Cultural norms and traditions, however, imposed gender roles that hindered the eradication of gender-based discrimination. Women had less representation in local politics, community associations, and in parliament. In the private sector, women held fewer management and leadership positions and often received lower salaries than men for equal work.

Indicators showed women faring better than men in terms of educational achievement, life expectancy, and access to sexual and reproductive health services. The government enforced the law in providing for the same legal status and rights for women as for men.

Children

Birth Registration: Citizenship can be derived by birth within the country or from one's parents. The government has a network of services, such as notary and civil identification records offices in all municipalities, and the Birth Registration Project located in hospitals and health centers. Failure to register births did not result in denial of public services. The government attributed the nonregistration of births to uncertainty as to the identity of fathers, parental neglect, and a lack of information on registration in the poorest communities.

Education: The government provided tuition-free and universal education for all children between the ages of six and 12. Education is compulsory until the age of 15. Secondary education was free only to children whose families had an annual income below 147,000 escudos ($1,482).

Child Abuse: Violence against children remained a problem. The government tried to combat it through a national network that included the Cabo Verdean

Institute of Childhood and Adolescence (ICCA), various police forces, the Attorney General's Office, hospitals, and health centers. The government attempted to reduce sexual abuse and violence against children through several programs such as Dial a Complaint, the Children's Emergency Program, Project Our House, Welcome Centers for Street Children, Project Safe Space, Project Substitute Family, and the creation during 2014 of five ICCA offices.

Data from the Children's Emergency Program and the Local Social Service programs indicated that during the first six months of the year, there were 126 reported cases of violence and aggression and 72 reported cases of sexual abuse of children. Actual prevalence was higher; not every case was reported because perpetrators were often relatives of the child.

<u>Early and Forced Marriage</u>: The legal minimum age of marriage is 18 years.

<u>Sexual Exploitation of Children</u>: The law punishes those that foment, promote, or facilitate prostitution or sexual exploitation of children age 16 and under with a penalty of four to 10 years in prison. If the victim is age 17 to 18, the penalty is two to six years in prison, which is inconsistent with international law on trafficking in persons. The law punishes those that induce, transport, or provide housing or create the conditions for sexual exploitation and prostitution of children age 16 and under in a foreign country with a penalty of five to 12 years in prison. If the victim is age 17 to 18, the penalty is two to eight years in prison. The law prohibits the use of children under 18 in pornography, with penalties of up to three years in prison. The minimum age for consensual sex is 14. The law also prohibits pedophilia. During the year there were no reported cases of child pornography, but there were cases of children in prostitution. Sex tourism, at times involving children in prostitution, was a problem, particularly on the tourism-focused islands of Sal and Boa Vista. Sexual abuse was more common in the poorest neighborhoods. Children were exploited in sex trafficking in Santa Maria, Praia, and Mindelo.

New amendments to the penal code, published in November 2015, increase penalties for those who engage in the sexual abuse and exploitation of minors or promote the prostitution of minors. These amendments also strengthen penalties for sexual assault, with imprisonment of two to eight years; sexual abuse of children, with penalties from two to eight years; and sexual abuse of minors between 14 and 16 years old, with penalties from two to eight years. Prison sentences increased for the crimes of pimping and the exploitation of minors for pornographic purposes. The new amendments also focus on crimes related to trafficking in persons, penalizing those who offer, deliver, accept, carry, or accommodate a child or other person for the purpose of sexual exploitation, labor exploitation, or extraction of organs. The amendments mandate several penalties, ranging from one to 12 years in prison for such crimes. Despite the amendments, there were no confirmed cases, prosecutions, or arrests related to trafficking in persons during the year.

The government also continued efforts to prevent the sexual exploitation of children through the creation of a national coordinating committee and the development of a code of ethics for the tourism industry.

Institutionalized Children: During the year there were reports of physical abuse of children in a foster care facility managed by the Reformed Congregation of Seventh-day Adventists in Praia. Eight children who spent time at this orphanage were transferred to ICCA's Children Emergency Center in Praia. The eight minors, six male and two female, were between ages seven and 17. All children were expected to remain at the ICCA center until an investigation was completed.

International Child Abductions: The country is not a party to the 1980 Hague Convention on the Civil Aspects of International Child Abduction. See the Department of State's *Annual Report on International Parental Child Abduction* at travel.state.gov/content/childabduction/en/legal/compliance.html.

Anti-Semitism

There is a very small Jewish community in the country, and there were no reports of anti-Semitic acts.

Trafficking in Persons

See the Department of State's *Trafficking in Persons Report* at www.state.gov/j/tip/rls/tiprpt/.

Persons with Disabilities

The law prohibits discrimination against persons with physical, sensory, intellectual, and mental disabilities in employment, education, access to health care, the judicial system, or in the provision of other state services. The law does not prohibit discrimination in air travel or other transportation services. The government generally enforced these provisions, with problems remaining in a number of areas. For example, persons with disabilities faced daily obstacles that hindered their integration. Physical accessibility, communication means, and public transport appropriate for persons with disabilities often were lacking. The government worked with civil society organizations to implement programs to provide access for wheelchair users, including building ramps to enhance access to transportation and buildings.

According to the Ministry of Education, Family, Equality, and Inclusion, the ministry had enrolled an estimated 1,200 children and youth with special educational needs in primary, secondary, and higher education through the years. There was no information available regarding abuse of persons with intellectual or mental disabilities in prisons or psychiatric hospitals. Persons with physical disabilities had difficulties in accessing facilities in prisons such as bathrooms and other services. Inmates with mental disabilities did not have access to psychiatric care or specific therapy. The government did not legally restrict the right of persons with physical disabilities to vote or otherwise participate in civic affairs and public life, unless the person was deemed not to have the mental capacity to exercise that right. Persons with intellectual or mental disabilities, as determined by the Ministry of Health, are not allowed to vote, according to the National Commission for Elections. According to the electoral code, blind persons or those with other physical disabilities that are not otherwise accommodated can be escorted by a citizen of their choice to cast their vote.

The government has a quota system for granting scholarships and tax benefits to companies that employ individuals with disabilities. NGOs recognized these measures as partially effective in better integrating these citizens into society but also noted nonenforcement and inadequate regulations continued to be obstacles.

Several NGOs worked to protect the interests of persons with disabilities. A Law on Mobility sets technical standards for accessibility for persons with disabilities for a variety of public facilities and services.

The Ministry of Education, Family, Equality, and Inclusion is the government organization responsible for protecting the rights of persons with disabilities. The National Council on the Status of Disabled Persons works in partnership with the ministry as a consultative body responsible for proposing, coordinating, and monitoring the implementation of a national policy.

Public television station TCV, through a partnership with the National Commission for Human Rights and Citizenship, Handicap International, and the Cabo Verdean

Federation of Associations of People with Disabilities, included in its nightly news a sign-language interpreter for deaf persons able to sign.

The law stipulates a quota of 5 percent of educational scholarships be allocated to persons with disabilities, but this percentage had not been reached.

Acts of Violence, Discrimination, and Other Abuses Based on Sexual Orientation and Gender Identity

Antidiscrimination laws exist, and state employers may not discriminate based on sexual orientation. There was no information available on official or private discrimination against lesbian, gay, bisexual, transgender, and intersex (LGBTI) individuals in employment, occupation, housing, statelessness, or access to education or health care.

There were no reported incidents of violence against LGBTI persons during the year.

In June the Arco Iris Association, in partnership with the Fundacion Triangulo of Spain, organized the country's fourth consecutive Cabo Verdean Gay Week ("Mindelo Pride"). The event again occurred in the city of Mindelo, on Sao Vicente Island, to promote equality and respect for sexual diversity. In June a smaller pride week event also took place in Praia, the first time an organized pride event had been held in the capital.

In December 2015 the United Nations launched in Cabo Verde the "Free and Equal" campaign to promote educational programs to shape public attitudes about LGBTI equality and increase awareness about homophobic violence and discrimination.

Section 7. Worker Rights

a. Freedom of Association and the Right to Collective Bargaining

The law provides for the rights of workers to form or join unions of their choice without previous authorization or excessive requirements, to engage in collective bargaining, and to conduct legal strikes. The labor code provides for protection against antiunion discrimination and for the reinstatement of workers. Although government enforcement generally was effective, cases could continue for years, with further delay for appeals. The Directorate General for Labor (DGT) has a conciliation mechanism to promote dialogue.

The labor code designates certain jobs essential and limits workers' ability to strike in those industries. Services provided by telecommunications, justice, meteorology, health, firefighting, postal service, funeral services, water and sanitation services, transportation, ports and airports, private security, and the banking and credit sectors are considered indispensable. The Civil Need Law states the government can force the end of a strike when there is an emergency or "to ensure the smooth operation of businesses or essential services of public interest." The law allows unions to carry out their activities without interference.

Freedom of association and the right to collective bargaining were respected, and the government effectively enforced applicable laws. The government protected the right to carry out union activities without interference. Worker organizations were independent of the government and political parties. There were no reports of violence, threats, or other abuses during the year by the government against union members or leaders. Penalties were adequate to deter violations of freedom of association. There was no reported evidence of antiunion discrimination. Nonetheless, public projects were contracted to private companies who hired workers directly. Workers who do not have a labor contract have no legal protection.

Labor unions complained the government sporadically restricted the right to strike for certain critical job categories. Other observers stated the government cooperated with the unions and did not discriminate against certain job categories. There were no reported violations related to collective bargaining. According to the local press, few companies had adopted collective bargaining, but the International Labor Organization worked with local unions and government bodies to provide guidance on conducting a dialogue between parties.

b. Prohibition of Forced or Compulsory Labor

The law prohibits all forms of forced or compulsory labor, including by children, and the government effectively enforced applicable laws. According to the Inspectorate General of Labor (IGT) 2015 Report, the IGT carried out 904 inspections and did not identify any forced labor violations. Article 14 of the labor code prohibits forced labor, and Article 271 of the penal code outlaws slavery, both of which prescribe penalties of six to 12 years of imprisonment, which was usually sufficiently stringent to deter violations.

Nevertheless, there were reports such practices occurred during the year. Migrants from China, Guinea-Bissau, Senegal, Nigeria, and Guinea may receive low wages and work without contracts, creating vulnerabilities to forced labor in the construction sector. Children labored in domestic service, often working long hours and at times experiencing physical and sexual abuse, indicators of forced labor (see also section 7.c.).

Also see the Department of State's *Trafficking in Persons Report* at www.state.gov/j/tip/rls/tiprpt/.

c. Prohibition of Child Labor and Minimum Age for Employment

The legal minimum age for work is 15 years. The labor code does not allow children ages 15 to 18 to work more than 38 hours a week or more than seven hours a day. The constitution provides that underage children may work only on small household tasks, in apprenticeship or training programs, or to help support the family. Children ages 16 to 18 are allowed to work overtime in an emergency but may not work more than two overtime hours a day, and these extra hours may not exceed 30 hours a year. The law defines work to be abolished or the worst forms of child labor as work engaged in by children under the age of 15 and/or dangerous work performed by children between the ages of 15 and 17.

Several laws prohibit child labor, and the penalties they impose are adequate, but enforcement was neither consistent nor effective. Barriers, mostly cultural, remained to the effective implementation of these laws. For example, not all citizens considered children working to help support their families as a negative thing, especially in small remote communities.

The ICCA, DGT, and IGT worked on matters pertaining to child labor. The ICCA works on the promotion and defense of the rights of children and adolescents. The DGT creates labor market policy and drafts labor legislation to ensure the promotion of social dialogue and reconciliation between social partners. The IGT has the responsibility to monitor and enforce labor laws and enforces rules relating to labor relations. The agencies stated they had adequate resources. During the year the government (through the three agencies) continued to carry out training activities for local staff and awareness campaigns to combat child labor, particularly in its worst forms, and consulted with local businesses. The IGT did not identify any child labor violations.

The first survey conducted by INE on child labor in the country, published in 2013, revealed that 7.1 percent of children were engaged in the worst forms of child labor (the study was conducted between October and December 2012). The worst forms of child labor were more common in rural areas (91 percent) than urban areas (84 percent). Child labor was also higher for boys (8.8 percent) than girls (5.3 percent).

Children engaged in street work, including in water and food sales, car washing, and begging, and were vulnerable to trafficking. The worst forms of child labor included street work, domestic service, agriculture, fishing, animal husbandry, trash picking, garbage and human waste transport, and peddling drugs for adults. Cabo Verde is a source and destination country for children subjected to forced labor and sex trafficking within the country and in Guinea and a destination country for women in forced prostitution. Boys and girls, some of whom may be foreign nationals, were exploited in sex trafficking in Santa Maria, Praia, and Mindelo.

Also see the Department of Labor's *Findings on the Worst Forms of Child Labor* at www.dol.gov/ilab/reports/child-labor/findings/.

d. Discrimination with Respect to Employment and Occupation

The labor law prohibits discrimination in employment and occupation based on race, color, sex, gender, disability, language, sexual orientation, gender identity, political opinion, ethnic origin, age, HIV-positive status or having other communicable diseases, or social status, and the government in general effectively enforced the law.

Gender-based discrimination in employment and occupation, however, occurred (see section 6). Women generally had lower economic status and less access to management positions in public- and private-sector organizations. Women experienced inequality in areas such as politics and the economy. For instance, housework is not officially recognized, since national statistics consider homemakers inactive members of the labor force. Reportedly, in some sectors of the formal economy, women received lower salaries than men for equal work.

According to a study conducted by the INE in 2010, more than eight in 10 immigrants were active in the local economy, with a rate of 91 percent among Africans. African immigrants worked mainly in retail, services, and construction. Immigrants generally had low education and professional qualifications and little work experience; as a consequence, their wages tended to be lower. Most of these immigrants did not have a legal contract with the employer, and thus they did not enjoy many legal protections and often worked in unacceptable conditions.

e. Acceptable Conditions of Work

The law stipulates a minimum monthly wage of 11,000 escudos ($110.95). The government defines the poverty income level as 105 escudos ($1.05) a day. The law stipulates a maximum of eight hours of work per day and 44 hours per week. The law requires rest periods, the length depending on the work sector. The minimum rest period is 12 hours between workdays. The law also provides for daily and annual overtime hours granted in exceptional circumstances. The law states a worker is entitled to 22 business days of paid vacation. Overtime must be compensated with at least time and a half pay. The worker, however, can replace up to half of his/her holidays through an agreement with the employer.

The law sets minimum occupational and safety standards and gives workers the right to decline to work if working conditions pose serious risks to health or physical integrity. In specific high-risk sectors, such as fishing or construction, the government can and often does provide, in consultation with unions and employers, specific current and appropriate occupational safety and health rules. In general it is the employer's responsibility to ensure the workplace is secure, healthy, and hygienic. The employer must also develop a training program for workers. Workers can remove themselves from situations that endangered health or safety without jeopardy to their employment. Authorities effectively protected employees in these situations.

Standards were enforced in all sectors, including the informal sector, although no penalties for violations that included fines or imprisonment were imposed during the year. The government made efforts to reduce work accidents and illness at work by carrying out more inspections and awareness campaigns to promote a culture of prevention and safety at work. The DGT and IGT are charged with implementing labor laws. Seven technicians worked for the DGT and 14 worked for the IGT, covering three islands (Santiago, Sao Vicente, and Sal). Both agencies agreed with trade unions these numbers were inadequate, and there remained a need for tighter enforcement of labor standards, especially on the more sparsely populated islands where monitoring was more difficult. Even though companies tended to respect laws on working hours, many employees, such as domestic workers, health professionals, farmers, fishermen, and commercial workers, commonly worked for longer periods of time than the law allows.

Penalties for labor violations depend on the number of workers employed; the minimum is 10,000 escudos ($100) going up to 180,000 escudos ($1,815). According to the IGT, there were no penalties for violations during the year.

According to the IGT's 2015 report, most irregularities detected during labor inspections related to nonsubscription to Social Security, nonsubscription to Mandatory Insurance for Job Injury, and some irregularities in complying with health and safety standards. Inspections revealed the most common work violations concerned the right to vacation time and the right to rest periods between work periods. Specific data, however, on wages and hours of work was not available. Nonetheless, the report indicated the IGT made 904 inspections, and inspectors identified 1,622 irregularities across the nine islands in all sectors, of which 358 required intervention. Although there were no official studies available, some sources speculated foreign migrant workers were more likely to be exploited than others.

Between 17,000 and 22,000 immigrants, mostly from the Economic Community of West African States, were working in the country. Most were men, but the number of immigrant women recently increased. No official data existed, but most immigrants were between the ages of 20 and 40 and lacked higher job qualifications but played important roles in the economy. Generally they worked in civil construction, security services, hospitality, and tourism. It was common for companies not to honor migrant workers' rights regarding contracts, especially concerning deductions for social security.

No official data was available on the number of work-related accidents and workplace deaths during the reporting period. The restaurant business/food services, steel industry, and the construction sector had the most work accidents reported during the year.